50 Keto Desserts Recipes 2021

INTRODUCTION

Keto stands for "ketogenic diet," which is characterized by a high-fat, moderate-protein, and low-carbohydrate diet. The keto diet's basic principle is to compel your body to cease burning glucose for energy and instead burn fat. Carbohydrates are limited to 10% of daily dietary intake, whereas protein is only 20%. The rest is made up of fat.

Eating a high-fat, low-carb diet puts your body into "ketosis," a metabolic state in which your body burns fat instead of glucose for energy. Ketosis is thought to be the best state for losing weight. The ketogenic diet was created to help people with serious illnesses. The keto diet can help with cancer, PCOS, autism, and degenerative brain illnesses, including Alzheimer's and Parkinson's. For almost a century, the keto diet has been used to treat epilepsy.

Keto is the most recent diet craze. It's being used to "hack" the body to achieve speedier weight reduction, exercise, and body-sculpting gains, in addition to being utilized medically. According to the keto diet requirements, a keto dessert is heavy in fat, moderate in protein, and low in Carbohydrates.

According to the keto diet, a keto dessert is high in fat, moderate in protein and low in Carbohydrates. These all dessert recipes are made up from all common ketogenic dessert ingredients such as almond flour and coconut flour coconut cream, heavy whipping cream, unsweetened, shredded coconut

almond, peanut, berries, cranberries, lemon, and lime cacao powder and cocoa butter, etc. Dessert recipes are best to serve after dinner to your loving guests.

Table of Contents

INTRODUCTION 2

LOW CARB SUGAR-FREE CARAMEL SAUCE 6

KETO SEA SALT CARAMEL ICE CREAM BARS 8

KETO MAPLE SYRUP 10

ALMOND RICOTTA CHEESE COOKIES 12

KETO CAKE POPS 14

HEALTHY GLUTEN-FREE BLUEBERRY CRISP - LOW CARB 17

DARK CHOCOLATE THICK MILKSHAKE 19

IRISH CREAM NO-BAKE CHEESECAKE 21

KETO WHIPPED CREAM 23

HEALTHY CHOCOLATE ZUCCHINI COOKIES 25

EGG FAST SUGAR-FREE MERINGUE COOKIES 27

KETO COFFEE COOKIES 29

KETO HAYSTACK COOKIES 31

DAIRY-FREE GLUTEN-FREE PUMPKIN COOKIES WITHOUT EGGS 33

GLUTEN-FREE KETO GINGER SNAPS COOKIES 36

GLUTEN-FREE THUMBPRINT COOKIES WITH JAM 38

KETO MOLTEN LAVA CAKE 40

CREAM CHEESE DARK CHOCOLATE KETO FUDGE 42

CHOCOLATE KETO BISCOTTI 44

COCONUT CHEESECAKE WITH COCONUT CREAM 46

KETO BLUEBERRY ICE CREAM 48

KETO LOW CARB PECAN PIE 50

HEALTHY KETO PUMPKIN CUSTARD 52

EASY LEMON COCONUT CUSTARD PIE WITH COCONUT MILK 54

LOW CARB KETO TIRAMISU 56

SUGAR-FREE TOOTSIE ROLLS 59

KETO MOCHA CHEESECAKE 61

KETO CREME BRULEE 64

SUGAR-FREE KETO GUMMY BEARS 66

SUGAR-FREE WHITE CHOCOLATE BARS 68

SUGAR-FREE DRIED CRANBERRIES 70

HOMEMADE KETO CHOCOLATE BARS 72

GLUTEN-FREE KETO STRAWBERRY RHUBARB CRISP	74
MASCARPONE CREAM MOUSSE DESSERT - KETO	76
RED WHITE AND BLUE CHEESECAKE SALAD DESSERT	78
SUGAR-FREE FUDGESICLES FUDGE POPS	80
LOW CARB GLUTEN FREE BLUEBERRY COBBLER	82
LEMON COCONUT CREAM CHEESE BALLS	84
LOW CARB COCONUT MACAROONS	86
ITALIAN ALMOND MACAROONS -KETO	88
HOMEMADE SUGAR-FREE PEPPERMINT PATTIES	90
MINT CHOCOLATE CHIP FUDGE	92
EASY GREEN TEA ICE CREAM - NO EGGS	94
CHAYOTE SQUASH MOCK APPLE PIE	96
KETO YELLOW SQUASH CAKE	99
BUCHE DE NOEL – YULE LOG CAKE	101
KETO JICAMA APPLE FILLING	104
STRAWBERRY ALMOND MILK CHIA PUDDING	106
CRANBERRY EGGPLANT BREAD PUDDING	108
SIMPLE LOW CARB SUNDAE	110

LOW CARB SUGAR-FREE CARAMEL SAUCE

Prep Time: 5 Minutes

Cook Time: 10 Minutes

Serves: 4

A low-carb caramel sauce that is sweet and salty with only 1 gram of total Carbohydrates per tablespoon. There's also no sugar, alcohol, or fiber sweetener in this recipe.

Nutrition

Calories: 194 | Carbohydrates: 2g | Fiber: 1g | Sugar: 1g | Saturated Fat: 4g

Cholesterol: 20mg | Sodium: 6mg | Potassium: 11mg

Ingredients

- ⅛ teaspoon Lakanto vanilla liquid monk fruit sweetener more or less to taste
- ¼ cup unsalted butter use salted if you like salty caramel
- 1 tablespoon almond butter, preferably unsalted
- ¼ cup heavy cream

Instructions

1. Butter should be melted in a pan over medium heat until golden brown and frothy. It's better to start with a light-colored pan so you can keep an eye on the color.
2. To the browned butter, add the heavy cream and almond butter. To include, stir everything together. Reduce the heat to low and constantly stir until the sauce has thickened. Add a dash of salt or more to taste if using unsalted butter or almond butter that hasn't been salted.
3. Remove the pan from the heat and add the sweetness drops. It's better to use it right away because it hardens as it cools and must be gently reheated before reusing.

KETO SEA SALT CARAMEL ICE CREAM BARS

Prep Time: 30 Minutes

Cook Time: 15 Minutes

Chill Time: 6 Hours

Serves: 12

These keto sea salt caramel ice cream bars are incredibly simple to make and have a delicious flavor. They're so low-carb you won't believe it

Nutrition

Calories: 290 | Carbohydrates: 7g | Protein: 1g | Fat: 20g | Saturated Fat: 17g

Polyunsaturated Fat: 1g | Fiber: 23g | Sugar: 1g | Cholesterol: 70mg

Ingredients

- 1 large egg
- ¼ cup coconut oil
- 2 cups heavy cream
- 7 ounces ChocZero Dark Chocolate Chips
- ¾ cup ChocZero Caramel Syrup
- ¾ teaspoon sea salt or pink Himalayan salt
- 1 tablespoon vanilla extract

Instructions

1. Heavy cream, egg, vanilla extract, caramel syrup, and sea salt are whisked together in a medium pot. Cook over medium heat, constantly stirring, until the mixture begins to steep, being careful not to boil. Place the mixture in a heat-safe mixing bowl and chill for one to two hours to cool. Place the bowl in the freezer for ten to fifteen minutes to speed up the cooling process.
2. After the mixture has a cold, remove it from the refrigerator. Whip for three to five minutes with an electric mixer to incorporate as much air as possible. Add popsicle sticks to the batter and divide them into ice cream pop molds. Freeze for at least four hours or until completely solid.
3. Freeze two baking sheets coated with silicone mats or parchment paper. In a chocolate Melter, double boiler, or microwave, melt the coconut oil and chocolate chips together, being careful not to burn them. Removed the cooled baking sheets with parchment paper from the freezer. Dip each ice cream bar into the melted chocolate, allowing the coating to firm somewhat before placing on the baking pans lined with parchment paper. Freeze the dipped bars for thirty to sixty minutes to firm the chocolate fully.
4. In the freezer, keep bars wrapped in micro popsicle bags or in an airtight container. Frozen ice cream bars should last at least six months in the freezer. Any remaining chocolate coating can be poured into molds and refrigerated.

KETO MAPLE SYRUP

Prep Time: 10 Minutes

Cook Time: 10 Minutes

Serves: 16

There are no net Carbohydrates in this keto maple syrup recipe. It's a low-carb, low-sugar topping for keto pancakes, waffles, and chaffles.

Nutrition

Calories: 3 | Carbohydrates: 1g | Fiber: 1g | Sugar: 1g | Sodium: 7mg | Calcium: 1mg

Ingredients

- 2 cup warm water divided
- 1 cup Swerve brown sugar substitute
- 1 ½ tablespoons maple extract
- 1 teaspoon vanilla extract
- 1 teaspoon xanthan gum

Instructions

1. In a small bowl, combine 1/2 cup of warm water and the xanthan gum. Whisk constantly and quickly until the mixture has thickened and is completely blended.
2. In a saucepan over medium heat, combine the remaining water and the sugar substitute. When the mixture is heated, stir in the xanthan gum mixture until smooth and completely incorporated. Allow the syrup to thicken to your preferred consistency.
3. Remove the maple and vanilla extracts from the heat and stir them into the syrup mixture. Allow it to cool before serving or storing in an airtight jar in the refrigerator.

ALMOND RICOTTA CHEESE COOKIES

Prep Time: 7 Minutes

Cook Time: 20 Minutes

Serves: 32

Although these low-carb ricotta almond biscuits are delicious on their own, the sugar-free almond paste on top adds a particular touch. It's also gluten-free.

Nutrition

Calories: 76 | Carbohydrates: 2g | Protein: 2g | Fat: 7g | Saturated Fat: 2g | Fiber: 1g

Sugar: 1g | Trans Fat: 1g | Cholesterol: 14mg

Ingredients

- ⅔ cup low carb sugar substitute
- 2 teaspoons vanilla extract
- 1 teaspoon almond extract
- 1 teaspoon baking powder
- ½ cup butter
- ⅔ cup ricotta cheese
- ½ teaspoon baking soda
- 1 egg

Icing

- ½ cup Swerve Confectioners Powdered Sweetener or powdered erythritol
- ½ teaspoon almond extract
- 2 tablespoons almond milk

Instructions

1. Cream together butter, sweetener, eggs, ricotta cheese, and extracts in a mixing dish.
2. Combine the almond flour, baking powder, and baking soda in a separate bowl.
3. Mix the dry flour mixture into the creamed mixture until it forms a dough.
4. Using a cookie dough scoop, drop onto a Silpat-lined baking sheet. To avoid the cookie dough scoops being too flat, I recommend chilling them for ten to fifteen minutes before baking.
5. Bake at 350°F for fifteen to eighteen minutes, or until gently browned. Allow them to cool on the baking sheet at least fifteen minutes before removing them because they are fragile when warm. Place cookies on racks to cool entirely if necessary. Store cookies in the refrigerator.

Icing

1. Combine almond milk, powdered erythritol, and almond extract in a mixing bowl and whisk until smooth.
2. To frost the cookies, use a brush or a drizzle.

KETO CAKE POPS

Prep Time: 30 Minutes

Cook Time: 30 Minutes

Chill Time: 2 Hours

Serves: 15

Enjoy these keto cake pops at your next party or get-together with only 3g net Carbohydrates per pop! They're also great for satisfying sudden sweet cravings. This cake pop recipe is for chocolate cake pops, but there are instructions for making other flavors as well.

Nutrition

Calories: 165 | Carbohydrates: 7g | Fiber: 13g | Sugar: 1g | Protein: 4g | Fat: 11g

Saturated Fat: 7g | Cholesterol: 64mg

Ingredients

- 4 large eggs
- 6 tablespoons heavy cream
- ½ cup unsweetened cocoa powder
- 2 teaspoons coconut oil melted
- 9 ounces ChocZero White Chocolate Baking Chips
- 3 tablespoons coconut flour
- ¼ cup ChocZero Chocolate Syrup
- ¼ cup low carb sweetener
- 2 teaspoons vanilla extract
- 2 teaspoons baking powder
- keto sprinkles optional

Instructions

1. Preheat the oven to 325 degrees Fahrenheit. Grease an 8-inch baking pan lightly. Line the bottom of the pan with parchment paper to make the cake easier to remove.
2. Whisk together cocoa powder, coconut flour, sweetener, and baking powder in a large mixing bowl.
3. Mix the heavy cream, melted coconut oil, and vanilla extract in a mixing bowl. Add the eggs one at a time, beating with an electric mixer after each addition.
4. Transfer cake batters to prepared pan and bake for twenty-five to thirty minutes, or until cake tests are done, in a preheated oven. A toothpick inserted towards the center should come out dry, and when softly pressed, the top should spring back. Place the cake on a wire rack to cool fully.
5. Cut the cake into squares and place them in a large mixing dish. Using your hands or a fork, crumble the cake pieces into fine crumbs. Choc Zero Chocolate Syrup is uniformly mixed into the crumbs to moisten them and allow them to be molded into balls.
6. Melt the white chocolate entirely in a chocolate Melter or double boiler while forming the balls. It's best to use a chocolate Melter to keep the chocolate warm while the balls are cooling in the freezer. However, you can melt them in the microwave in fifteen to thirty seconds intervals on a lower power setting, being cautious not to burn the chocolate.
7. Measure out roughly 2 teaspoons of the cake mixture with a cookie scoop or a spoon. Form a ball with the mixture in your hands and lay it on a parchment-lined sheet pan. Rep till the entire mixture is shaped into balls. In total, you should have roughly 15 balls.
8. Dip the very top of each cake pop stick into the melted white chocolate, then insert it into the center of a cake ball. Rep with the rest of the sticks and cake balls. Place the cake

balls in the freezer for one to two hours, or until they are completely frozen. If possible, keep the melted chocolate warm.
9. Remelt the chocolate if necessary, in a double boiler or microwave, being careful not to burn it. To coat each cake ball, dip it into the melted chocolate. As the chocolate hardens, rotate the cake pop stick to keep the chocolate uniformly distributed over the cake ball. If you're using sprinkles, do so as soon as possible, so they attach to the chocolate before it solidifies.
10. To allow the chocolate to set completely, insert the stick into the Styrofoam block once it has hardened to the point where it will not drip. To coat each cake ball with chocolate, repeat the process. To solidify the chocolate-coated balls fast, place them in the refrigerator or freezer.
11. Once the chocolate has hardened completely, put the cake pops in an airtight container in a cool location. Alternatively, wrap each one in a clear treat bag and keep it in cups with a twist tie.

HEALTHY GLUTEN-FREE BLUEBERRY CRISP - LOW CARB

Prep Time: 5 Minutes

Cook Time: 35 Minutes

Serves: 8

A delicious low-carb blueberry crisp with pecans and coconut flour on top. For a delightful gluten-free dessert, serve it warm and topped with ice cream.

Nutrition

Calories: 125 | Carbohydrates: 9g | Protein: 1g | Fat: 8g | Saturated Fat: 2g | Fiber: 4g

Sugar: 8g | Cholesterol: 8mg | Sodium: 88mg

Ingredients

<u>Filling</u>

- ¼ cup low carb sugar substitute
- 4 cups blueberries fresh or frozen
- ½ teaspoon cinnamon
- 1 teaspoon vanilla extract
- 1 teaspoon xanthan gum
- ⅛ teaspoon nutmeg

<u>Topping</u>

- 2 tablespoons coconut flour or almond flour
- 1 tablespoon low carb sugar substitute
- ½ teaspoon ground cinnamon
- ½ cup pecans finely chopped
- 2 tablespoons butter
- dash nutmeg

Instructions

1. Fill a 1/2-quart baking dish halfway with the filling ingredients.
2. Mix pecans, coconut flour, sweetener, cinnamon, and nutmeg in a mixing bowl. Using a pastry cutter, cut in the butter and then sprinkle over the blueberry mixture.
3. Preheat oven to 350°F and bake for thirty-five minutes.
4. Warm, with ice cream or whipped cream on top.

DARK CHOCOLATE THICK MILKSHAKE

Prep Time: 10 Minutes

Cook Time: 0 Minutes

Serves: 2

It's simple to make thick homemade milkshakes that rival those seen at fast food establishments. This low-carb dark chocolate frosty milkshake is thick and delicious.

Nutrition

Calories: 302 | Carbohydrates: 2.5g | Fiber: 6.8g | Sugar: 1.3g | Protein: 4.8g

Fat: 27.1g | Saturated Fat: 19.5g | Cholesterol: 62mg

Ingredients

- ⅛ teaspoon vanilla extract
- 5 tablespoon canned coconut milk
- 6 tablespoons heavy whipping cream
- 2 tablespoons unsweetened dark cocoa powder
- 2 tablespoons low carb sugar substitute or other sugar substitutes

Instructions

1. Whip the cream with an electric mixer until soft peaks form.
2. Add the remaining ingredients in a slow, steady stream.
3. Continue to pound until you get stiffer peaks.
4. Place the mixture in the freezer.
5. Remove from freezer after twenty minutes and mix with a fork to break up any frozen patches around the edges.
6. Check and stir the mixture every twenty minutes until it reaches the desired consistency.

IRISH CREAM NO-BAKE CHEESECAKE

Prep Time: 15 Minutes

Cook Time: 2 Minutes

Chill Time: 2 Hours

Serves: 8

This wonderful low-carb no-bake Irish cream cheesecake will appeal to coffee and chocolate enthusiasts. This delicious dessert can be made in little size or in a big pan.

Nutrition

Calories: 522 | Carbohydrates: 5g | Fiber: 2.2g | Cholesterol: 123mg | Protein: 6.5g

Fat: 42.4g | Saturated Fat: 23.8g | Sodium: 168mg

Ingredients

<u>Crust</u>

- 2 Tablespoons low carb sugar substitute
- 2 ½ Tablespoons cocoa
- ¾ cup almond flour
- 3 Tablespoons butter

<u>Filling</u>

- 2 teaspoons vanilla extract
- 1 teaspoon grass-fed gelatin
- 1 cup heavy whipping cream
- ⅓ cup low carb sugar substitute
- 8 ounces cream cheese
- ½ cup low carb Irish cream
- 3 tablespoons butter
- 3 tablespoons cocoa
- 2 teaspoons cold water, 2 teaspoons hot water
- 2 tablespoons Swerve Confectioners Powdered Sweetener

Instructions

<u>Crust</u>

1. Combine the almond flour, cocoa, and sweetener in a small mixing dish.
2. Add the melted butter and divide the mixture among eight 4-ounce jars or dessert cups.
3. Make a crust at the bottom of each cup by pressing down.

<u>Filling</u>

1. In a microwave-safe mixing bowl, combine cream cheese and butter. At high power, cook for one minute.
2. With an electric mixer, blend the cocoa, sweetener, Irish cream, and vanilla extract until smooth. Set aside.
3. Whip heavy cream with sweetener in a separate mixing dish until soft peaks form.
4. Sprinkle gelatin over cold water in a small cup until softened. Stir in the boiling water until it is completely dissolved. Whip the heavy cream until stiff peaks form, then gradually add the dissolved gelatin. Whip until the mixture is firm. Fold the whipped cream into the cream cheese mixture gently. Fill dessert bowls with the mixture by piping or spooning them in. Refrigerate for at least two hours before serving. If desired, top with whipped cream and shaved chocolate.

KETO WHIPPED CREAM

Prep Time: 5 Minutes

Cook Time: 0 Minutes

Serves: 4

This keto whipped cream recipe is so simple to create that you'll be able to use it in any keto dessert you make. Each serving has only 1 g of net carbohydrates.

Nutrition

Calories: 106 | Carbohydrates: 2g | Protein: 1g | Fiber: 0.4 | Sugar: 1g | Fat: 11g

Saturated Fat: 7g | Cholesterol: 41mg | Sodium: 11mg

Ingredients

- 1 teaspoon Vanilla extract
- ½ cup Heavy whipping cream
- 3 tablespoons Swerve Confectioners' sugar substitute
- Pinch nutmeg optional
- Pinch cinnamon optional

Instructions

1. In a mixing dish, combine all of the ingredients.
2. Beat on high speed until firm peaks emerge. If you overwhip the mixture, it will turn into butter instead of cream.

HEALTHY CHOCOLATE ZUCCHINI COOKIES

Prep Time: 15 Minutes

Cook Time: 15 Minutes

Serves: 12

Are you looking for a new low-carb dessert? These healthy double chocolate cookies are a must-try. They're a tasty way to get more veggies into your diet or use up a garden crop.

Nutrition

Calories: 140 | Carbohydrates: 5g | Protein: 3g | Fat: 13g | Fiber: 3g | Sugar: 0g

Saturated Fat: 7g | Cholesterol: 15mg | Sodium: 116mg

Ingredients

- ½ cup Lakanto Golden Monk Fruit Granular Sweetener or raw honey for paleo
- ¼ cup cacao powder or unsweetened cocoa powder
- ⅓ cup butter flavored coconut oil or ghee
- 1 cup zucchini grated or shredded
- ½ teaspoon baking soda
- ¼ cup coconut flour
- 1 cup almond flour
- ¼ teaspoon cinnamon
- 1 teaspoon vanilla extract
- ½ teaspoon salt
- 1 large egg yolk
- ¼ cup sugar-free chocolate chips or dark chocolate pieces (optional)

Instructions

1. Zucchini can be grated or shredded. Squeeze out the excess liquid by wrapping it in a towel. Continue to absorb liquid while wrapped in a towel.
2. Combine almond flour, coconut flour, cacao powder, baking soda, salt, and cinnamon in a small mixing bowl. Set aside.
3. Melt the coconut oil or ghee in a large glass mixing dish. Add the sweetener and toss to combine. The egg yolk and vanilla extract are then whisked in.
4. In a large mixing bowl, combine the zucchini and the sweetened mixture. Then add the dry ingredients and mix well. If using, fold in the chocolate.
5. Roll the dough into 1 tablespoon-sized ball by hand. Flatten each ball and, if preferred, top with a few pieces of chocolate.
6. Preheat oven to 350°F and bake for ten-twelve minutes, or until golden brown.

EGG FAST SUGAR-FREE MERINGUE COOKIES

Prep Time: 10 Minutes

Cook Time: 120 Minutes

Serves: 48

If you're on an Egg Fast, you might be looking for a snack. These stevia-sweetened sugar-free meringue cookies contain almost no Carbohydrates, making them keto-friendly.

Nutrition

Calories: 6 | Protein: 1.1g | Carbohydrates: 0.1g

Ingredients

- ¼ teaspoon + ⅛ teaspoon cream of tartar about 1.27 grams
- ¾ teaspoon Sweet Leaf stevia drops
- 5 egg whites

Instructions

1. Preheat the oven to 215 degrees Fahrenheit.
2. Line two cookie sheets with parchment paper.
3. Cream the egg whites with the cream of tartar until soft peaks form.
4. While continuing to whip the egg whites, gradually add the stevia until stiff peaks form.
5. Drop beaten egg whites onto the prepared cookie sheets in drops.
6. Bake for about two hours or until the edges of the cookies start to brown.
7. Allow cookies to brown in a heated oven until the desired color is achieved.

KETO COFFEE COOKIES

Prep Time: 5 Minutes

Cook Time: 20 Minutes

Serves: 11

Every coffee lover's dream comes true with these fluffy sugar-free keto coffee biscuits! They're dangerously wonderful; the espresso flavor shows through in every bite of these keto cookies, and the chocolate on top adds a nice sweet note.

Nutrition

Calories: 176 | Carbohydrates: 4g | Fiber: 2g | Sugar: 1g | Saturated Fat: 4g

Protein: 5g | Fat: 16g | Cholesterol: 44mg

Ingredients

- 2 eggs, in-room temperature
- 2 cups almond flour
- 3 teaspoon espresso coffee
- 2 teaspoon vanilla extract
- ½ teaspoon baking soda
- ⅓ cup swerve
- ⅓ cup butter

Toppings

- 1 teaspoon sliced almond
- 1 teaspoon unsweetened chocolate chopped

Instructions

1. Add the vanilla extract to the eggs in a mixing bowl and stir with an electric whisk.
2. Whisk in the sugar, coffee, and melted butter.
3. With a spatula, combine the almond flour and baking soda with the rest of the ingredients.
4. Using parchment paper, line a baking tray.
5. Scoop the batter into the baking dish, leaving space between the cookies to allow for expansion.
6. Flatten the tops of each cookie with a spatula, then sprinkle chopped unsweetened chocolate on half of them and sliced almond on the other half.
7. Preheat the oven to 170°C and bake for twenty minutes.
8. Allow time for the cookies to cool before serving.

KETO HAYSTACK COOKIES

Prep Time: 10 Minutes

Cook Time: 15 Minutes

Chill Time: 15 Minutes

Serves: 14

The perfect low-carb sweet, keto haystack cookies! These no-bake keto cookies are prepared with peanut butter and coconut shreds and take only 30 minutes to prepare.

Nutrition

Calories: 145 | Total Fat: 7.4g | Carbohydrates: 4.6g | Fiber: 2.4g | Sugar: 1.2g

Protein: 3.5g | Net Carbohydrates: 2.2g

Ingredients

- 1 1/2 cups shredded unsweetened coconut
- 3 tablespoons Confectioners' Swerve
- 1/4 teaspoon pure vanilla extract
- 2/3 cup natural unsalted peanut butter
- 2 tablespoons coconut oil
- Pinch of fine sea salt

Instructions

1. Over medium-low heat, heat a medium non-stick skillet. Allow the coconut oil to melt before adding it.
2. Stir in the vanilla essence and Confectioners' Swerve with a silicone spatula until everything is well mixed.
3. Stir in half of the peanut butter until it melts and is well integrated. Rep with the rest of the peanut butter.
4. Add the salt and mix it in.
5. In a large mixing bowl, sift the shredded coconut. Pour the liquid ingredients over the coconut shreds and mix until they are uniformly covered.
6. Using parchment paper, line a baking sheet.
7. Using a cookie scoop, scoop the dough onto the baking sheet. This recipe should yield 14 cookies.
8. Freeze the cookies for fifteen minutes or until they are completely set.

DAIRY-FREE GLUTEN-FREE PUMPKIN COOKIES WITHOUT EGGS

Prep Time: 10 Minutes

Cook Time: 15 Minutes

Serves: 30

It's hard to think that autumn is only a few months away. It's the ideal time to bake some delicious low-carb pumpkin cookies.

Nutrition

Calories: 43 | Carbohydrates: 1g | Saturated Fat: 1g | Protein: 1g | Fiber: 0g | Sugar: 0g

Fat: 3g | Cholesterol: 0mg

Ingredients

- 2 tablespoons room temperature water
- ½ cup low carb sugar substitute
- ¼ cup coconut oil
- 1 cup almond flour
- ½ teaspoon baking powder
- ½ teaspoon baking soda
- 1 tablespoon grass-fed gelatin
- ½ teaspoon cinnamon
- ¼ cup coconut flour
- ½ cup pumpkin puree
- ½ teaspoon vanilla extract
- ¼ teaspoon ginger
- ⅛ teaspoon cloves
- ½ teaspoon sea salt
- ¼ cup hot water

Optional Glaze

- ¼ teaspoon vanilla
- 1 tablespoon unsweetened almond milk
- 5 tablespoons Swerve Confectioners Powdered Sweetener

Instructions

1. In a small mixing bowl, combine almond flour, coconut flour, baking soda, baking powder, cinnamon, ginger, cloves, and salt. Set aside.
2. Combine coconut oil, pumpkin puree, and vanilla essence in a medium mixing bowl. Set aside.
3. In a separate mixing dish, combine 2 tablespoons of room temperature water and gelatin. Allow for a five-minute rest period.
4. Take 14 cups hot water and whisked into gelatin mixture until gelatin is completely dissolved. Beat in the granular low-carb sweetener until the mixture is light and fluffy.
5. Using an electric mixer, blend the pumpkin mixture with the frothy gelatin mixture.
6. Blend the dry ingredients into the pumpkin mixture gradually.
7. Drop a rounded spoonful of dough onto greased or parchment-lined baking sheets. Use your fingertips to gently press down.

8. Preheat oven to 350°F and bake for twelve to fifteen minutes. Before removing the cookies from the pan, let them cool fully. You can put them in the refrigerator to expedite the process.
9. If you're going to use the glaze, whisk together all of the glaze ingredients in a small dish and drizzle over the cookies.
10. Refrigerate cookies in an airtight container.

GLUTEN-FREE KETO GINGER SNAPS COOKIES

Prep Time: 15 Minutes

Cook Time: 10 Minutes

Serves: 21

Do you enjoy ginger? These low-carb, gluten-free ginger cookies are soft and chewy. They're comparable to gingersnaps but without the crunch.

Nutrition

Calories: 128 | Carbohydrates: 6g | Fiber: 2g | Sugar: 1g | Protein: 2g | Fat: 11g

Cholesterol: 25mg | Saturated Fat: 5g | Sodium: 98mg

Ingredients

- 1 egg
- ¾ cup Sukrin Gold or other brown sugar substitutes
- 1 ½ cups almond flour
- 2 teaspoons baking powder
- 2 teaspoons ground ginger
- ¾ teaspoon ground cinnamon
- ½ teaspoon ground cloves
- ¾ cup coconut flour
- ¼ teaspoon salt
- ¾ cup butter softened
- 2 tablespoons low carb sugar substitute optional
- 1 tablespoon Sukrin Gold Fiber Syrup optional

Instructions

1. Combine almond flour, coconut flour, baking powder, ginger, cinnamon, cloves, and salt in a large mixing bowl.
2. Cream butter and Sukrin Gold together in a separate large mixing dish.
3. In a mixing bowl, whisk together the butter and Sukrin Gold Fiber Syrup if using.
4. Slowly incorporate the dry ingredients into the butter mixture. Make a dough by kneading the ingredients together.
5. If preferred, scoop into balls and roll in Sukrin:1.
6. Place dough balls or scoops on a parchment paper-lined cookie sheet or a non-stick silicone baking sheet with a 1 1/2-inch gap between them. With a flat bottom glass, press each ball down.
7. Preheat oven to 350 degrees Fahrenheit and bake for eight to ten minutes.

GLUTEN-FREE THUMBPRINT COOKIES WITH JAM

Prep Time: 15 Minutes

Cook Time: 15 Minutes

Serves: 36

With a dollop of raspberry jam on top, this is a slightly sweet shortbread cookie. This gluten-free cookie is one you'll want to bake all year.

Nutrition

Calories: 85 | Carbohydrates: 5g | Fiber: 2.1g | Fat: 8.3g| Sodium: 23.1mg

Ingredients

- 2 egg yolks
- 3 tablespoons Pyure All-Purpose or 6 tablespoons Swerve
- 1 teaspoon sugar-free vanilla extract
- 1 ⅓ cup almond flour fine ground
- ½ cup coconut oil liquified
- 1 batch of chia raspberry jam
- 1 teaspoon xanthan gum
- ½ cup butter melted
- ⅔ cup coconut flour

Instructions

1. Preheat the oven to 350 degrees Fahrenheit. Use parchment paper or a silicone mat to line a cookie sheet.
2. Mix coconut oil, butter, sweetener, yolks, and vanilla in a large mixing bowl.
3. Start with half a cup of coconut flour and add more if necessary. Coconut flour absorbency varies, and using too much can result in dry, crumbly biscuits. Stir half of the coconut flour, all of the almond flour, and the optional xanthan gum in a mixing bowl until a dough form. If necessary, add more coconut flour.
4. Scoop dough balls onto a prepared cookie sheet in an equal layer.
5. Make an indentation on the top of each cookie with the tip of your finger.
6. Fill each divot in the biscuit with chia raspberry jam.
7. Preheat oven to 350°F and bake for twelve to fifteen minutes.

KETO MOLTEN LAVA CAKE

Prep Time: 10 Minutes

Cook Time: 15 Minutes

Serves: 2

On the first bite, gooey melting chocolate oozes out of this wonderful low-carb molten lava cake. It's a keto-friendly treat that's both simple and decadent.

Nutrition

Calories: 240 | Carbohydrates: 5g | Protein: 9g | Fiber: 4g | Sugar: 1g | Fat: 21g

Saturated Fat: 10g | Cholesterol: 195mg

Ingredients

- 3 tablespoon Swerve confectioners' sugar substitutes
- 2 tablespoon Unsalted Butter melted
- ¼ cup Unsweetened cocoa powder
- 2 large eggs at room temperature
- 1 tablespoon Almond flour
- ½ teaspoon Vanilla extract
- ½ teaspoon Baking powder

Instructions

1. Preheat the oven to 350 degrees Fahrenheit.
2. Combine the ingredients in a mixer bowl and beat on high until smooth and creamy.
3. Pour the batter evenly into two 6-ounce ramekins that have been properly buttered.
4. Bake for twelve-fifteen minutes, or until the cake's edges are firm, but the center still jiggles slightly.
5. Allow it cool for a few minutes before turning out onto a plate to serve.
6. If preferred, top with sugar-free whipped cream.

CREAM CHEESE DARK CHOCOLATE KETO FUDGE

Prep Time: 5 Minutes

Cook Time: 10 Minutes

Serves: 16

This delectable cream cheese chocolate fudge will satisfy your sweet craving. With only 3 grams of Carbohydrates per large square, it's a wonderful low-carb treat.

Nutrition

Calories: 259 | Carbohydrates: 5g | Cholesterol: 46mg | Protein: 4g | Fiber: 2g

Sugar: 1g | Fat: 26g | Saturated Fat: 11g

Ingredients

- 1 cup Swerve Confectioners Powdered Sweetener SukrinMelis or Swerve Confectioners
- 1-ounce unsweetened baking chocolate can add 2 ounces to up flavor
- 1 cup unsweetened almond butter or peanut butter, or sun butter
- 1 teaspoon stevia concentrated powder
- ⅓ cup unsweetened cocoa powder
- 1 teaspoon vanilla extract
- 8 ounces cream cheese
- 1 cup butter see note

Instructions

1. Using parchment paper, line an 8x8 baking sheet.
2. Melt the butter, baking chocolate, and cream cheese together over medium heat
3. With an electric mixer, whip in the almond butter
4. Remove the pan from the heat and whisk in the rest of the dry ingredients. To integrate as thoroughly as possible, use an electric mixer. After that, add the vanilla extract.
5. Evenly distribute the ingredients in the prepared pan. Refrigerate until ready to use.

CHOCOLATE KETO BISCOTTI

Prep Time: 10 Minutes

Cook Time: 50 Minutes

Serves: 15

A simple recipe for gluten-free, low-carb chocolate biscotti cookies. With a cup of coffee, these delicate chocolate Italian style cookies are w Ingredients

Nutrition

Calories: 82 | Carbohydrates: 4g | Cholesterol: 20mg | Protein: 3g | Fiber: 2g

Fat: 7g | Saturated Fat: 2g | Sodium: 112mg

Ingredients

- 1 large egg
- ¼ teaspoon stevia concentrated powder or 2½ tablespoons sugar substitute
- ¼ cup erythritol or 3 tablespoons sugar substitute
- ½ cup unsweetened cocoa
- ½ teaspoon vanilla extract
- ¼ cup of butter softened
- ¼ teaspoon xanthan gum
- 1 ¾ cups almond flour
- ½ teaspoon baking soda
- 1 teaspoon cinnamon
- ¼ teaspoon sea salt
- chopped nuts (optional)
- sugar-free chocolate chips (optional)

Instructions

1. Preheat the oven to 325 degrees Fahrenheit. Mix butter, granular sweetener, stevia, egg, and vanilla in a mixing bowl until well combined. Combine all of the dry ingredients in a separate bowl and stir until well blended. Mix the dry and wet ingredients and stir until completely combined. Chocolate chips or nuts can be added at this point if desired.
2. Make a huge dough ball out of the mixture. Place the dough ball on a silicone baking mat or a cookie sheet lined with parchment paper. Make a low, flat log out of the dough.
3. Bake for twenty minutes, or until the dough is gently browned and cake-like. Remove the baking sheet from the oven and lower the temperature to 275 degrees F. Cool the log for about ten minutes before slicing it into 12-inch-wide thin strips. Place the slices on the cookie sheet on their side and bake for about twenty-thirty minutes, or until fully crisped.

COCONUT CHEESECAKE WITH COCONUT CREAM

Prep Time: 15 Minutes

Cook Time: 90 Minutes

Chill Time: 60 Minutes

Serves: 16

A low-carb and keto-friendly cheesecake that's simple and tasty. It's a simple coconut cream dessert to create.

Nutrition

Calories: 207 | Carbohydrates: 4g | Cholesterol: 48mg | Protein: 4g | Fiber: 1g | Sugar: 0g

Fat: 20g | Saturated Fat: 11g | Sodium: 69mg

Ingredients

Crust

- 3 tablespoons low carb sugar substitute
- 1 ½ cups almond flour
- ½ cup butter melted
- 1 teaspoon cinnamon

Filling

- 3 large eggs
- 32 ounces cream cheese or four 8-ounce blocks
- 1 teaspoon vanilla extract or coconut extract
- ½ can of coconut cream 13.5-ounce size
- ¾ cup low carb sugar substitute

Frosting

- ¼ cup Swerve Confectioners Powdered Sweetener or SukrinMelis
- ½ can of coconut cream 13.5-ounce size
- 2 tablespoons cream cheese softened

Instructions

1. Mix the ingredients for the crust and press onto the bottom of a 9-inch springform pan. While preparing the filling, keep it refrigerated.
2. Put the filling ingredients in a large mixing bowl just till the mixture is smooth.
3. Fill the crust with the filling and bake for fifteen minutes at 350°F. Reduce the oven temperature to 250°F and continue baking for another seventy-five to ninety minutes.
4. Place in the refrigerator to cool fully. Remove the springform side of the cake by running a knife along the edge.
5. To make the frosting, whisk the coconut cream, powdered sugar, and cream cheese in a mixing bowl until smooth.
6. Using a spatula, frost the cooled cake. Before slicing, chill for at least one hour.

KETO BLUEBERRY ICE CREAM

Prep Time: 10 Minutes

Cook Time: 45 Minutes

Serves: 8

On hot summer days, treat yourself to a scoop of this delightful ice cream. Coconut cream is used to make a low-carb, sugar-free, and dairy-free dessert.

Nutrition

Calories: 185 | Carbohydrates: 4.5g | Fat: 14g | Fiber: 10.8g

Protein: 1.2g | Sodium: 43mg

Ingredients

- 1 lime
- 13.5 oz coconut cream
- ⅓ cup unsweetened almond milk or coconut milk
- ⅔ cup LC Foods white sweetener – inulin
- ½ teaspoon xanthan gum optional
- 1 cup blueberries

Instructions

1. Grate the lime zest finely and squeeze the juice into a medium saucepan.
2. In a mixing bowl, whisk the cream layer from the canned coconut cream until stiff peaks form.
3. Pour the coconut cream's liquid portion into a saucepan with the lime.
4. Mix the sweetener, blueberries, and low-carb milk in a mixing bowl.
5. Bring to a boil, then reduce to low heat and simmer for four minutes, stirring regularly.
6. Remove from the heat and, if using, mix in the xanthan gum. Allow it cool for a few minutes before folding in the whipped coconut cream.
7. Refrigerate or ice bath the mixture until it is completely cooled.
8. Follow the manufacturer's instructions for ice cream making.

KETO LOW CARB PECAN PIE

Prep Time: 10 Minutes

Cook Time: 40 Minutes

Serves: 12

If you use the correct sweetener, you can make a tasty keto-friendly pecan pie. This traditional holiday pie is so tasty that you'll want to eat it all year.

Nutrition

Calories: 249 | Carbohydrates: 5.9g | Fiber: 3.7g | Cholesterol: 78mg Sugar: 1.1g

Protein: 5.1g | Fat: 23.4g | Saturated Fat: 23.4g

Ingredients

Crust

- 2 eggs
- ¼ cup low carb sugar substitute leaves out for savory crust
- ½ cup coconut flour sifted
- ½ cup almond flour
- ¼ cup butter melted
- ¼ teaspoon salt

Filling

- 2 eggs
- ¼ cup allulose powdered sweetener or regular granular sweetener
- ½ cup Sukrin Fiber Syrup Gold or ChocZero Caramel Sugar-Free Syrup
- ¼ cup butter melted
- 1 ½ cup chopped pecans
- 2 teaspoons vanilla extract
- ½ teaspoon salt

Instructions

Crust

1. In a medium microwavable bowl, melt the butter.
2. Combine almond flour, eggs, sweetener (if using), and salt in a mixing bowl. Mix thoroughly. In a separate bowl, sift the coconut flour.
3. Knead the dough for one minute with your hands, then roll it into a ball.
4. Roll out dough to an 18-inch thickness between wax paper and fit into a 9-inch pie pan or roll directly into the pie dish with a tiny pastry roller.

Filling

1. In a large mixing bowl, whisk together the eggs, sugars, butter, vanilla, and salt until thoroughly combined.
2. Pour into pie crust after adding chopped pecans.
3. Preheat the oven to 325°F and bake for thirty-five to forty minutes, or until a toothpick inserted halfway between the middle and the crust comes out clean. The pie should not be totally set in the middle.
4. Allow it to cool slightly before serving. Leftovers can be kept in the refrigerator for up to a week.

HEALTHY KETO PUMPKIN CUSTARD

Prep Time: 5 Minutes

Cook Time: 40 Minutes

Serves: 6

You may still enjoy fall delicacies if you avoid dairy and sugar. Check out this low-carb, keto-friendly custard with a pumpkin flavor.

Nutrition

Calories: 160 | Carbohydrates: 6g | Protein: 3g | Fiber: 2g | Sugar: 2g | Cholesterol: 122mg

Fat: 13g | Saturated Fat: 10g

Ingredients

- 4 large egg yolks
- 1 teaspoon Lakanto liquid monk fruit sweetener or liquid stevia
- 15 ounces pumpkin puree 425 grams
- ¾ cup coconut cream heat to liquefy if needed
- ¼ teaspoon ginger
- ⅛ teaspoon cloves
- 1 teaspoon cinnamon

Instructions

1. Preheat the oven to 350 degrees Fahrenheit.
2. In a large mixing dish, combine the pumpkin, sugar, cinnamon, ginger, and cloves.
3. In a separate bowl, whisk together the egg yolks until fully combined.
4. Stir in the coconut cream slowly.
5. Fill individual ramekins with the ingredients.
6. Preheat oven to 350°F and bake for thirty-forty minutes, or until firm. Allow it to cool completely on a wire rack before refrigerating.

EASY LEMON COCONUT CUSTARD PIE WITH COCONUT MILK

Prep Time: 10 Minutes

Cook Time: 45 Minutes

Serves: 8

A low-carb, keto-friendly custard pie with coconut and lemon flavors. To make it a basic crustless pie, you don't have to make a crust.

Nutrition

Calories: 209 | Carbohydrates: 6g | Protein: 3g | Fat: 19g | Saturated Fat: 16g

Cholesterol: 54mg | Fiber: 3g | Sugar: 1g | Sodium: 35mg

Ingredients

- 2 large eggs can use 3 for stiffer custard
- 2 tablespoons unsalted butter melted and cooled
- 4 Ounces Unsweetened Shredded Coconut
- 1 cup Coconut Milk canned
- ¾ teaspoon baking powder
- 1 teaspoon vanilla extract
- ¼ cup coconut flour
- 1 teaspoon lemon zest
- ½ Teaspoon Lemon Extract

Instructions

1. Preheat the oven to 350 degrees and coat a 9-inch pie dish with cooking spray.
2. Mix the eggs, coconut milk, sweetener, coconut flour, butter, baking powder, vanilla, lemon zest, and lemon essence together in a large mixing bowl. Stir until everything is well blended.
3. Add the unsweetened coconut and mix well. Fill the pie dish halfway with the mixture.
4. Bake for forty to forty-five minutes, or until the edges are golden brown and the top is golden.
5. Remove the cake from the oven and set it aside to cool completely before cutting and serving.
6. Leftovers can be kept in the fridge for up to three days.

LOW CARB KETO TIRAMISU

Prep Time: 30 Minutes

Cook Time: 30 Minutes

Serves: 8

A low-carb version of a delectable gluten-free tiramisu. The dish is sweetened with stevia and erythritol, while the cake layer is created using almond flour.

Nutrition

Calories: 428 | Carbohydrates: 6g | Fiber: 1g | Sugar: 4g | Protein: 14g | Fat: 42g

Saturated Fat: 22g | Polyunsaturated Fat: 2g | Cholesterol: 324mg | Sodium: 103mg

Ingredients

Cake

- 3 large eggs
- 2 tablespoons powdered erythritol
- ½ teaspoon baking powder
- ⅛ teaspoon stevia extract powder
- ¼ teaspoon sugar-free vanilla extract
- ¼ teaspoon almond extract
- ⅛ teaspoon cream of tartar
- ½ cup almond flour
- Unsalted butter
- ⅛ teaspoon salt

Custard

- 6 egg yolks
- ⅛ teaspoon stevia extract powder or stevia glycerite
- 2 tablespoons powdered erythritol
- 1 ¾ cups heavy or whipping cream
- 1-2 tablespoons rum or brandy
- 8 ounces mascarpone cheese
- ¼ cup strong coffee or espresso
- 1 teaspoon vanilla extract optional
- ½ teaspoon coffee extract optional

Instructions

Cake

1. Preheat the oven to 350 degrees Fahrenheit. Butter a 117-inch baking dish. Re-grease with butter after lining with parchment paper.
2. Combine the almond flour, baking powder, and salt in a large mixing bowl.
3. Remove the eggs from the shells. Beat the yolks and sweeteners with an electric mixer until thick and lemon-colored. Combine the vanilla, almond extract, and cream of tartar in a bowl and mix. Fold in the almond flour
4. To make firm peaks, whip the egg whites with a clean bowl and beaters. Stir ¼ into the almond mixture. F. 1/2 of the remaining whites are folded in until barely blended, and then the final 1/2 are folded in until thoroughly incorporated. In the prepared pan, spread evenly.

5. Preheat the oven to 350°F and bake for fifteen-twenty minutes, or until the top springs back when lightly pushed. Allow it to cool.

Custard

1. Whisk together egg yolks, erythritol, and stevia in a small mixing bowl until thick and lemon-colored.
2. Place the mixture over boiling water on the top of a double boiler. Reduce the heat to a low setting. Cook for eight-ten minutes while constantly stirring. Remove the pan from the heat. In a separate bowl, whisk the mascarpone cheese until smooth.
3. In a small mixing bowl, beat heavy or whipping cream until stiff peaks form. Incorporate the egg yolk mixture. If desired, add vanilla and/or coffee extract. Set aside some time

Assembly

1. Make 16 fingers out of the almond cake.
2. In a small bowl, combine the rum and espresso.
3. Coat the bottom of a 9-inch bread pan with cocoa powder, then line with half of the almond cake fingers.
4. Lightly coat the cake fingers in the espresso mix with a brush, being careful not to get them too wet. Spread on ½ of the mascarpone mixture and dust the top with cocoa. Carry on with the layering. Finish with a sprinkling of cocoa.
5. Refrigerate overnight, covered.

SUGAR-FREE TOOTSIE ROLLS

Prep Time: 15 Minutes

Cook Time: 1 Minute

Serves: 3

Sweetened with stevia and an all-natural high-fiber sweetener, these nutritious homemade tootsie rolls are simple to make. You won't believe how sugar-free they are.

Nutrition

Calories: 90 | Fat: 5.4g | Carbohydrates: 3.6g | Protein: 3.6g | Fiber: 8.4g

Sodium: 63.6mg

Ingredients

- 60 grams Sukrin Fiber Syrup or another Oligosaccharide syrup
- 2 tablespoons powdered whole milk
- ½ cup low carb sugar substitute powdered
- ¼ cup unflavored whey protein
- teaspoon pinch salt about ⅛
- ½ teaspoon vanilla extract
- 2 tablespoons butter melted
- ¼ cup cocoa

Instructions

1. In a blender or food processor, finely grind the granular sweetener.
2. In a medium mixing bowl, combine chocolate, whey protein powder, powdered milk, low carb sweetener, and salt. Set aside.
3. Microwave the fiber syrup until bubbles form about 30 seconds. Pour in the melted butter and the vanilla extract.
4. Mix the dry cocoa powder with the moist fiber syrup until it's crumbly. Knead the contents with your hands until a dough form.
5. Form the dough into a ball and flatten it out. Cut the dough into strips and roll each strip into a rope the diameter of a Tootsie roll. Cut the dough rope into pieces the size of Tootsie Rolls.
6. If desired, wrap each roll in little rectangular pieces of wax paper. Rolls should be kept in the refrigerator to keep them firm.

KETO MOCHA CHEESECAKE

Prep Time: 10 Minutes

Cook Time: 115 Minutes

Serves: 12

To impress your low-carb pals, make this luscious sugar-free mocha cheesecake. The crust is prepared from gluten-free chocolate biscotti that has been crushed up.

Nutrition

Calories: 215 | Carbohydrates: 3.4g | Cholesterol: 106mg | Fiber: 4.1g | Sugar: 1g

Protein: 5.3g | Fat: 19.6g | Saturated Fat: 11.1g | Sodium: 177mg

Ingredients

<u>Crust</u>

- 2 packets of stevia or other low carb sweeteners
- 1 cup low carb chocolate biscotti finely ground
- 4 tablespoons butter melted

<u>Filling</u>

- 4 large eggs
- 32 packets stevia about 1 ⅓ cups sugar equivalent
- 4 ounces unsweetened chocolate melted
- 24 oz cream cheese 3 (8 ounces) packages
- 3 teaspoons instant espresso powder
- 1 ½ tablespoons coconut flour
- 1 cup sour cream

<u>Topping</u>

- 4 packets of stevia or other low carb sweeteners
- 1 teaspoon instant espresso powder
- 1 ½ cups sour cream

<u>Optional</u>

- cocoa powder for dusting
- sugar-free chocolates for decorating

Instructions

1. On the bottom rack of the oven, place a roasting pan filled with several inches of water.
2. Preheat the oven to 325°F. Using cooking spray, coat the bottom and sides of a 9-inch springform pan. Place the top oven rack in the oven's center.
3. Combine the chocolate biscotti crumbs, sweetener packets, and melted butter in a mixing bowl. The mixture must be pressed into the bottom of the prepared pan.
4. Set aside 3 teaspoons of espresso powder and 2 teaspoons of water.
5. On medium speed, beat the cream cheese with 32 packets of sweetener 1 1/3 cup sugar equivalent until light and fluffy. One at a time, add the eggs, beating well after each addition. Combine 1 cup sour cream and the coconut flour in a mixing bowl. Mix until everything is well blended. In a large mixing bowl, combine the espresso/water combination and the melted chocolate. Spread the mixture on top of the crust.

6. Bake for about one hour at 325 degrees F, or until the middle is set but jiggles slightly. Turn the oven off and leave the cake in the oven for twenty-five minutes with the door shut.
7. Combine the remaining 1 1/2 cup sour cream, the 4 packets of sugar, and 1 teaspoon espresso powder while the cheesecake is baking. After the twenty-five minutes are up, spread the mixture over the cheesecake and return it to the oven to cool it for another five minutes with the door closed. Remove the dish from the oven.
8. Cool the cake on a wire rack after running a sharp knife over the edges. Refrigerate the cake for at least eight hours or up to overnight. Remove the cake from the pan and sprinkle with cocoa powder or sugar-free chocolates to finish.

KETO CREME BRULEE

Prep Time: 15 Minutes

Cook Time: 35 Minutes

Serves: 2

Enjoy a sugar-free custard with a caramelized sweetener on top. With only 4 net carbohydrates, it's a delectable, low-carb treat.

Nutrition

Calories: 475 | Carbohydrates: 4g | Sugar: 1g | Cholesterol: 357mg | Protein: 5g

Fat: 49g | Saturated Fat: 29g | Sodium: 54mg

Ingredients

- 2 Egg Yolks
- 3 tablespoon Swerve confectioners' sugar substitutes
- 2-3 tablespoon Swerve granulated sweetener
- 1 C. Heavy whipping cream
- ¼ tablespoon Almond extract
- 1 tablespoon Vanilla extract
- Mini kitchen torch

Instructions

1. Preheat oven to 350 degrees Fahrenheit.
2. Add the heavy whipping cream and confectioners' sugar substitute to a pot over medium heat on the stove. To combine the ingredients, whisk them together.
3. Remove the cream mixture from the heat after it has reached a simmer.
4. In a mixing bowl, whisk together two egg yolks, vanilla extract, and almond extract until thoroughly blended.
5. Slowly pour the egg yolk mixture into the cream mixture, whisking constantly.
6. Evenly divide the mixture between two ramekins.
7. Create a water bath by placing the ramekins in a casserole dish with a little water in the bottom.
8. Bake for thirty minutes, or until the creme brulee's custard has set in the center.
9. Allow the crème Brulee to cool to room temperature before serving.
10. Before serving, sprinkle 1-2 tablespoons of granulated sugar on top of each creme Brulee and use a kitchen torch to caramelize and firm it to a crust.

SUGAR-FREE KETO GUMMY BEARS

Prep Time: 10 Minutes

Cook Time: 15 Minutes

Serves: 12

Here's how to make keto-friendly gummy bears at home, which are low-carb fruit snacks. These adorable candies are also high in gelatin, which is good for you.

Nutrition

Calories: 15 | Carbohydrates: 0g | Cholesterol: 0mg | Sugar: 0g | Protein: 4g

Fat: 0g | Saturated Fat: 0g | Sodium: 10mg

Ingredients

- 2 teaspoons pure fruit extract
- 4 bags herbal fruit tea
- ¼ cup low carb sugar substitute or Swerve
- 1 ⅓ cup hot boiling water

Instructions

1. Steep tea bags in hot boiling water for about six minutes.
2. Teabags will be squeezed out and discarded.
3. In a small saucepan, pour one cup of tea.
4. In a tea bowl, combine gelatin and sweetener.
5. On medium heat, heat and whisk the gelatin mixture until the liquid is thin and there are no gelatin clumps.
6. Take the pan off the heat and add the fruit extract.
7. Pour the mixture into silicone molds.
8. Refrigerate the filled molds for at least fifteen minutes.
9. Take the gummy candies out of the mold. Refrigerate the remaining ingredients.

SUGAR-FREE WHITE CHOCOLATE BARS

Prep Time: 5 Minutes

Cook Time: 10 Minutes

Serves: 6

It's quite simple to make your own low-carb white chocolate at home. It's a decadent delicacy that only has one net carb per serving.

Nutrition

Calories: 123 | Carbohydrates: 0.6g | Sugar: 0.2g | Saturated Fat: 8.1g

Fat: 13.2g | Sodium: 4mg

Ingredients

- 2.5 ounces cocoa butter food grade
- ½ teaspoon vanilla extract looks for one with no added sugar
- 1 tablespoon coconut milk powder or whey protein powder
- 3 tablespoons Swerve Confectioners Powdered Sweetener
- ⅛ teaspoon stevia concentrated powder
- ⅛ teaspoon monk fruit powder or extra stevia
- 1 teaspoon sunflower lecithin optional

Instructions

1. In a microwave, double boiler, or chocolate Melter, melt together cocoa butter, Swerve, coconut milk powder, lecithin, stevia, and monk fruit.
2. Remove from the heat and mix in the vanilla extract.
3. Fill molds with the mixture.
4. Refrigerate or freeze until the mixture is completely firm. Take it out of the mold.
5. Refrigerate covered until ready to use.

SUGAR-FREE DRIED CRANBERRIES

Prep Time: 10 Minutes

Cook Time: 12 Minutes

Serves: 6

Making your own low-carb dehydrated cranberries with keto-friendly sweeteners is straightforward. A dehydrator or a low-temperature oven can be used for drying.

Nutrition

Calories: 15 | Carbohydrates: 7g | Fiber: 1g | Sugar: 5g | Potassium: 43mg | Iron: 0.2mg

Ingredients

- 1 cup sugar substitute of your choice or 1 teaspoon stevia glycerite
- 1 bag fresh whole cranberries
- ½ cup water

Instructions

1. Preheat the oven to 200 degrees Fahrenheit.
2. Pick through the cranberries in a large skillet to remove any soft or brown ones. If the sweetener is powdered, mix it with water to dissolve it. Pour over the cranberries and whisk to combine.
3. Heat on high for four-five minutes, or until cranberries pop. If you wish to stop the cooking process early, use a toothpick for popping any extras. Every minute or two, give it a good stir. Turn off the burner and let them cool for ten minutes after they appear to have popped.
4. Using the back of a large spoon, squish them down. Allow for another five minutes to cool.
5. Three layers of paper towels and a piece of parchment paper will be used to cover the baking sheet. On the paper, spread the cranberries. As they dry, they will basically separate. If any remain un-popped, use a toothpick or mild pressure for popping them presently.
6. Place in oven and reduce heat to 150 degrees Fahrenheit or use a dehydrator set at 145F. Replace the parchment and flip the paper towels after two to four hours. If you're using a dehydrator, you can either turn the paper towels or just remove them once the moisture has been absorbed.
7. After six hours, begin checking. The total time is affected by humidity and other factors. It normally takes around 8 hours to complete. It also depends on whether you want them to be "crispier" or dry to the point where they still have some "give." Separate them and keep them in an airtight container.

HOMEMADE KETO CHOCOLATE BARS

Prep Time: 5 Minutes

Cook Time: 10 Minutes

Chill Time: 30 Minutes

Serves: 2

Pre-made low-carb chocolate is substantially more expensive than this homemade version. It's a simple dish made using keto-friendly natural sweeteners.

Nutrition

Calories: 112 | Carbohydrates: 4.5g | Protein: 2.5g | Cholesterol: 9mg | Fat: 11g | Fiber: 2g Sugar: 1g | Saturated Fat: 6g | Sodium: 8mg

Ingredients

- 1 tablespoon low-carb milk powder
- 4 ounces unsweetened baking chocolate chopped
- ¼ teaspoon monk fruit extract powder
- 1-ounce cocoa butter
- ½ teaspoon sugar-free vanilla extract
- 1 tablespoon powdered erythritol

Instructions

1. In a double boiler or chocolate Melter, melt the chocolate and cocoa butter together. Warm until the chocolate and cocoa butter are completely melted.
2. Mix in the powdered milk, stevia powder, and erythritol powder. Stir until the powdered components are completely dissolved, and the mixture is smooth. It may take some time for all of the erythritols to dissolve.
3. Remove the mold once it has hardened. Allow it to cool in the fridge or freezer. Store in an airtight container. If desired, it can also be kept in the refrigerator or freezer.

GLUTEN-FREE KETO STRAWBERRY RHUBARB CRISP

Prep Time: 10 Minutes

Cook Time: 30 Minutes

Serves: 4

Simple low-carb strawberry rhubarb crisp dish that takes only minutes to prepare. The ingredients can be combined directly in the bowl you'll be eating it from.

Nutrition

Calories: 164 | Carbohydrates: 6g | Protein: 2g | Fat: 15g | Fiber: 3g | Sugar: 3g

Cholesterol: 15mg | Saturated Fat: 4g | Sodium: 83mg

Ingredients

<u>Filling</u>

- 2 tablespoons low carb sugar substitute or 2 ½ teaspoons Truvia
- 1 ¼ cups diced rhubarb
- ½ teaspoon xanthan gum
- 1 ¼ cups sliced strawberries

<u>Topping</u>

- 1 tablespoon low carb sugar substitute or 1 ¼ teaspoon Truvia
- 4 teaspoons almond flour
- ½ teaspoon cinnamon
- ½ cup chopped pecans
- 2 teaspoons coconut flour
- 2 tablespoon butter
- dash nutmeg

Instructions

1. Combine the rhubarb, strawberries, sweeteners, and xanthan gum in a mixing bowl.
2. Fill a small baking dish halfway with the mixture.
3. Pecans, coconut flour, almond flour, sugar, cinnamon, and nutmeg will all be mixed together.
4. Cut the butter into small pieces and sprinkle over the fruit mixture.
5. Preheat oven to 350°F and bake for twenty to thirty minutes.
6. Warm, with ice cream or whipped cream on top.

MASCARPONE CREAM MOUSSE DESSERT - KETO

Prep Time: 10 Minutes

Cook Time: 0 Minutes

Serves: 12

Do you need a low-carb dessert quickly? Only three ingredients are needed to make this sugar-free mascarpone cheese mousse in under a minute! Served with berries, it's perfect

Nutrition

Calories: 158 | Carbohydrates: 4g | Protein: 5g | Fat: 15.8g | Cholesterol: 54mg

Fiber: 1g | Sugar: 3g | Saturated Fat: 9g

Ingredients

- 1 cup whipping cream
- 1-pint Berries
- 8 ounces mascarpone cheese
- ¾ teaspoon vanilla stevia drops

Instructions

1. In a large mixing dish, whisk together the mascarpone, cream, and sweetener with an electric mixer until well blended.
2. Using a pastry bag, pipe into individual cups and top with berries.

RED WHITE AND BLUE CHEESECAKE SALAD DESSERT

Prep Time: 10 Minutes

Cook Time: 0 Minutes

Serves: 23

A simple mixed berry salad is ideal for July 4th celebrations. It's a quick and easy dish that's red, white, and blue.

Nutrition

Calories: 134 | Carbohydrates: 6g | Protein: 2g | Fat: 11g | Fiber: 2g | Sugar: 5g

Cholesterol: 36mg | Saturated Fat: 6g

Ingredients

- 16 ounces strawberries cut into bite-sized pieces
- ¼ teaspoon stevia concentrated powder
- ½ teaspoon monk fruit concentrated powder
- 6 ounces raspberries about 1 cup
- 16 ounces cream cheese softened
- 1 cup heavy whipping cream
- 12 ounces blackberries about 2 cups
- 14 ounces blueberries about 4 cups

Instructions

1. Cream the cream cheese with an electric mixer until it is completely smooth.
2. Mix monk fruit, stevia, and heavy whipping cream in a mixing bowl. Using an electric mixer, beat until the mixture is thick and creamy. If the sauce becomes too thick, a bit more cream can be added.
3. In a large mixing bowl, combine the fresh berries and fold them in. Refrigerate or serve right away.

SUGAR-FREE FUDGESICLES FUDGE POPS

Prep Time: 5 Minutes

Cook Time: 10 Minutes

Chill Time: 6-8 Hours

Serves: 10

Frozen sweets are a great way to beat the heat. Here's how to create delicious keto-friendly low-carb Fudgesicles with only 5 grams of Carbohydrates. They're also dairy-free

Nutrition

Calories: 247 | Carbohydrates: 5g | Protein: 4g | Cholesterol: 0mg | Fat: 25g | Fiber: 5g

Sugar: 0g | Saturated Fat: 19g | Sodium: 31mg

Ingredients

- 3 tablespoons unsweetened cocoa powder or unsweetened cocoa
- ¾ cup almond milk or another low carb milk
- 1 teaspoon monk fruit liquid or ½ teaspoon stevia drops
- 8 ounces unsweetened baking chocolate
- 1 teaspoon vanilla extract
- 13.5 ounces coconut cream 1 can
- 2 tablespoons powdered erythritol or other powdered sweeteners (optional)

Instructions

1. In a medium saucepan, heat the coconut cream, almond milk, and cacao powder until hot.
2. In a separate bowl, melt the baking chocolate.
3. Remove from the heat and stir in the vanilla extract and sweetener drops. To taste, add powdered sweetener if desired.
4. Place in the freezer for thirty minutes after pouring into popsicle molds. Continue to freeze until the popsicle sticks are solid. Remove from the molds and set aside to defrost slightly before serving because they will freeze solid.

LOW CARB GLUTEN FREE BLUEBERRY COBBLER

Prep Time: 5 Minutes

Cook Time: 25 Minutes

Serves: 9

The season for blueberries has arrived. This is a low-carb cobbler with a gluten-free topping that tastes just like the genuine thing.

Nutrition

Calories: 103 | Carbohydrates: 5.9g | Cholesterol: 39mg | Protein: 1.1g | Fiber: 1.2g

Sugar: 4.9g | Fat: 8.3g | Saturated Fat: 5g | Sodium: 62mg

Ingredients

- 1 egg beaten
- ⅔ cup almond flour
- ⅓ cup coconut flour
- ¼ teaspoon xanthan gum
- 1 tablespoon lemon juice
- 3 cups blueberries fresh or frozen
- 6 tablespoons butter melted
- ¼ cup low carb sugar substitute adds more if needed

Instructions

1. Fill a greased 9x9-inch baking pan halfway with berries.
2. Lemon juice and xanthan gum are sprinkled on top. If desired, sweeten the blueberry combination with an extra 2-4 tablespoons of sugar.
3. Stir together almond flour, coconut flour, 14 cups granular sweetener, and egg until a coarse meal form.
4. Over the berries, sprinkle the dry mixture.
5. Pour melted butter over the topping.
6. Preheat oven to 350°F and bake for twenty-five minutes, or until the top is golden brown.

LEMON COCONUT CREAM CHEESE BALLS

Prep Time: 5 Minutes

Cook Time: 0 Minutes

Serves: 12

To fulfill a sweet desire, quick no-bake keto snacks are simple to create. These low-carb lemon coconut balls combine two delicious tastes into delicious cheesecake-like nibbles

Nutrition

Calories: 71 | Carbohydrates: 1g | Protein: 1g | Fat: 6g | Fiber: 0g | Sugar: 0g

Cholesterol: 10mg | Saturated Fat: 3g | Sodium: 31mg

Ingredients

- 2 tablespoons So Nourished Monk Fruit Erythritol blend
- 3 tablespoons shredded unsweetened coconut
- 2 to 3 tablespoons fresh lemon juice
- 4 ounces cream cheese softened
- ½ cup blanched almond flour

Instructions

1. In a food processor, combine the almond flour, cream cheese, monk fruit sweetener, and lemon juice.
2. Mix until a smooth dough forms, then roll into 12 balls by hand.
3. Place the balls on a baking sheet after rolling them in the coconut.
4. Chill until solid, then store in an airtight container in the refrigerator.

LOW CARB COCONUT MACAROONS

Prep Time: 10 Minutes

Cook Time: 12 Minutes

Serves: 20

Low-carb, sugar-free macaroon biscuits are great bite-sized treats. To make it even more decadent, drizzle it with melted chocolate.

Nutrition

Calories: 130 | Carbohydrates: 4g | Protein: 1g | Fat: 12g | Fiber: 3g | Sugar: 1g

Cholesterol: 18mg | Saturated Fat: 10g Sodium: 43mg

Ingredients

- ⅓ cup water
- 2 large eggs
- 3-4 cups unsweetened shredded coconut start with 3 cups, add more as needed
- ¾ cup low carb sugar substitute or less to taste
- ¾ teaspoon sugar-free vanilla extract
- sugar-free chocolate chips optional
- ¼ teaspoon sea salt

Instructions

1. Preheat the oven to 350 degrees Fahrenheit. Using a non-stick spray, lightly coat the baking sheet.
2. In a small saucepan, combine the water, low carb sweetener, salt, and vanilla extract and bring to a boil over medium-high heat. Remove the syrup from the heat after stirring it.
3. In a food processor, combine the egg and coconut flakes. Pour in the syrup and process until a dough form. Place mounds on a baking sheet about an inch apart, using a cookie scoop.
4. After eight minutes, rotate the baking pan in the oven. Bake for another four minutes, or until golden brown. Allow it to cool on a rack. If desired, drizzle with melted chocolate.

ITALIAN ALMOND MACAROONS -KETO

Prep Time: 10 Minutes

Cook Time: 60 Minutes

Serves: 45

Traditional gluten-free almond macaroons are quite simple to create. These low-carb cookies are great to share with friends and family.

Nutrition

Calories: 31 | Carbohydrates: 1g | Protein: 2g | Fat: 3g | Cholesterol: 0mg

Saturated Fat: 0g Fiber: 1g | Sugar: 0g

Ingredients

- 2 egg whites
- ½ teaspoon almond extract
- 2 tablespoons Lakanto powdered monk fruit sweetener
- ½ pound almond flour about 2 cups plus 2 tablespoons
- ¼ cup low carb sugar substitute

Instructions

1. Combine almond flour, white sugar, egg whites, and almond essence in a mixing bowl.
2. Knead the mixture with your hands until it forms a dough.
3. Make little balls out of the dough, about 1 inch in diameter.
4. Place balls at least 1 inch apart on a baking sheet lined with parchment paper.
5. Bake at 250°F for fifty-five to sixty minutes at the bottom of the oven.
6. While the cookies are still warm, transfer them to a wire rack and dust them with confectionery sweetness.

HOMEMADE SUGAR-FREE PEPPERMINT PATTIES

Prep Time: 15 Minutes

Cook Time: 15 Minutes

Serves: 15

Don't you have time to produce tasty low-carb confectionery at home? Reconsider your position. These delicious all-natural peppermint patties are simple to make.

Nutrition

Calories: 126 | Carbohydrates: 1g | Cholesterol: 9mg | Protein: 1g | Fat: 13g

Saturated Fat: 9g | Fiber: 1g | Sodium: 6mg

Ingredients

- ½ cup Swerve Confectioners Powdered Sweetener or powdered erythritol
- ½ teaspoon stevia glycerite or ¼ cup additional sweetener
- ½ cup coconut oil must be kind that gets solid in the fridge
- 2 teaspoons peppermint flavor or extract
- 1 ½ teaspoon non-hydrogenated shortening
- 4 ounces sugar-free chocolate chips
- 1 tablespoon heavy cream
- ½ teaspoon vanilla extract

Instructions

1. Wax paper, parchment paper, or a non-stick silicone mat is used to line two baking sheets.
2. Melt chocolate chips with shortening in a chocolate Melter or double boiler. After the chocolate chips have completely melted, keep it warm.
3. Combine the sweeteners and coconut oil in an electric mixer. You may need to reheat the coconut oil slightly before mixing it with the sweeteners if it is really hard. The extracts and cream are then added. It's best if the peppermint filling is a creamy paste.
4. Drop tablespoon-sized mounds onto one of the baking sheets prepared with the non-stick sheet, using a cookie scoop or spoon. With a knife or a spoon, gently flatten each mound.
5. Freeze the baking sheet for approximately minutes.
6. Place each frozen filling on the other lined baking sheet after dipping it in the chocolate. It's important to position the bumpy side down with the flat side up for better-looking chocolate-coated chocolates.
7. Refrigerate in an airtight container.

MINT CHOCOLATE CHIP FUDGE

Prep Time: 5 Minutes

Cook Time: 15 Minutes

Serves: 16

Only 0.7-gram net Carbohydrates per square in this sugar-free, low-carb mint chocolate chip fudge. It's a delicious treat that's suitable for individuals following a ketogenic diet.

Nutrition

Calories: 119 | Fat: 9.1g | Carbohydrates: 6.5g | Fiber: 3.5g | Protein: 4.1g

Sodium: 14mg

Ingredients

- 2 tablespoons water
- ½ teaspoon vanilla stevia drops
- 1 scoop unflavored whey protein 23 grams
- ¼ cup LC-Sweetened Condensed Milk mix
- ¾ cup sugar-free chocolate chips divided
- 1 teaspoon peppermint extract
- ¼ cup low carb sugar substitute
- 4 ounces cocoa butter
- ¼ cup heavy cream
- ½ teaspoon spinach powder optional

Instructions

1. Use parchment paper to line a small rectangular container. A 6x6 storage container was used.
2. Melt the cocoa butter, condensed milk mix, water, heavy cream, and Swerve sweetener in a double boiler bowl over a pan of simmering water.
3. Remove the bowl from the heat and stir in the stevia, whey protein powder, peppermint, and, if desired, spinach powder.
4. Allow it cool for a few minutes before folding in 1/2 cup of chocolate chips. As you fold, the chips should melt, forming chocolate swirls.
5. Fill the prepared container halfway with the fudge mix. Top with the remaining 1/4 cup of chocolate chips.
6. Refrigerate the fudge until it is hard. Squares should be cut off. Refrigerate leftovers in an airtight container.

EASY GREEN TEA ICE CREAM - NO EGGS

Prep Time: 10 Minutes

Cook Time: 30 Minutes

Serves: 5

A simple, sugar-free, low-carb green tea ice cream with a concentrated brewed tea flavor. This simple tea ice cream requires no eggs or an ice cream maker.

Nutrition

Calories: 249 | Carbohydrates: 2.1g | Fat: 25.6g | Protein: 1.5g | Sodium: 27mg

Ingredients

- ¼ cup Pyure all-purpose or ½ cup Swerve
- ½ cup unsweetened almond milk
- 1 ½ cup heavy cream
- ⅓ cup boiling water
- 4 green tea bags

Instructions

1. In a cup, combine tea bags and boiling water.
2. Allow for a five-minute steeping period.
3. Brew tea in boiling water. Squeeze tea from bags and discard.
4. In a cup of boiling tea, add a teaspoon of sugar. Allow it to cool before serving.
5. Combine the low-carb milk and cream in a mixing bowl.
6. Fill an ice cream machine canister halfway with the mixture and process according to the manufacturer's instructions.
7. It's best to eat it right after it's been frozen. Leftovers can be frozen, but they will need to be slightly thawed before serving.

CHAYOTE SQUASH MOCK APPLE PIE

Prep Time: 15 Minutes

Cook Time: 45 Minutes

Serves: 16

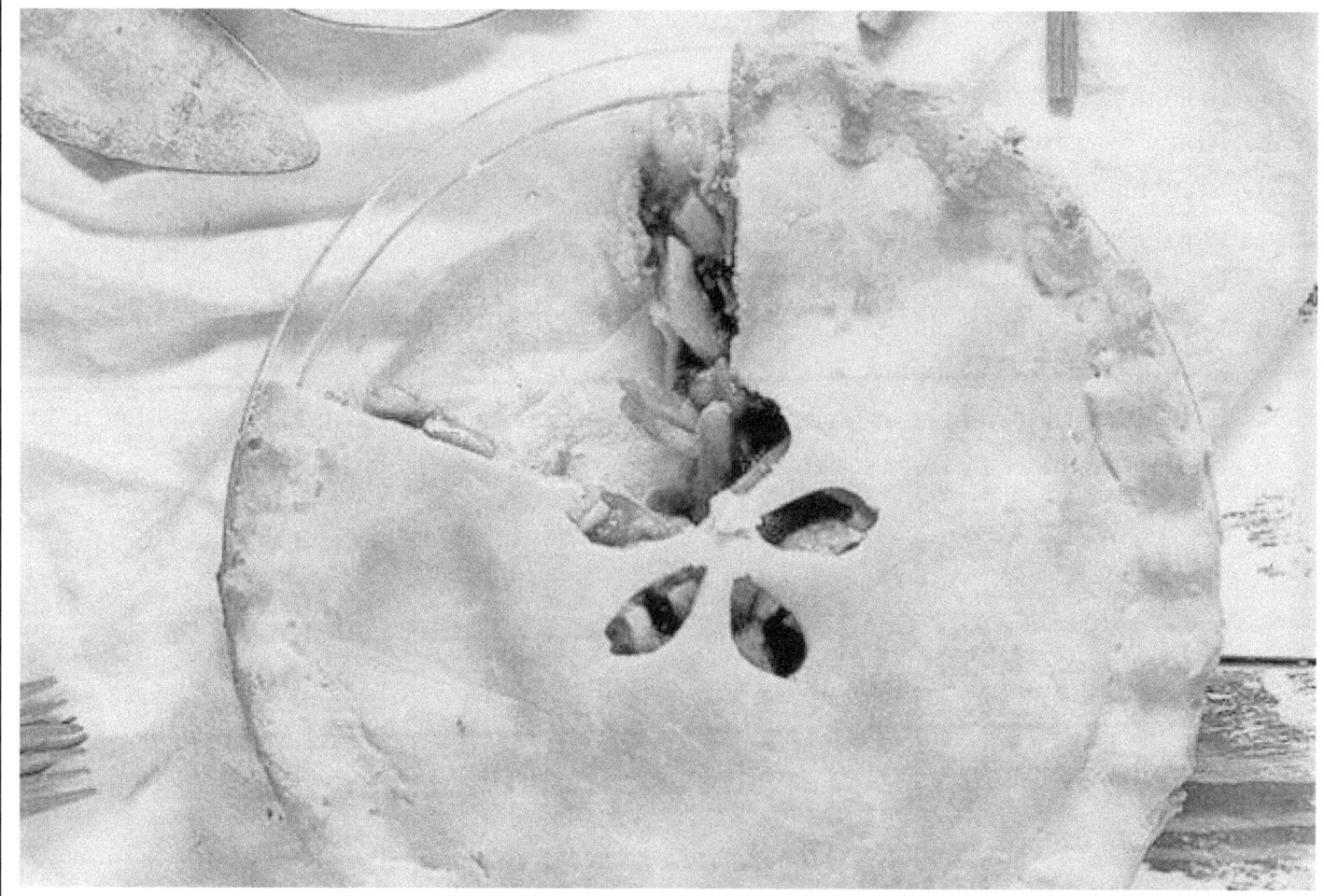

A wonderful low-carb faux apple pie made with chayote squash that tastes just like a genuine thing! Enjoy this delicious pie guilt-free. It's also gluten-free.

Nutrition

Calories: 187 | Carbohydrates: 6.6g | Cholesterol: 67mg | Protein: 2g | Fiber: 2.9g

Fat: 16.7g | Saturated Fat: 6.9g | Sodium: 204mg

Ingredients

Crust

- 4 eggs
- 1 tablespoon whole psyllium husks
- 1 ½ cup almond flour
- ½ cup butter melted
- ¾ cup coconut flour
- ½ teaspoon salt

Filling

- ¾ cup low carb sugar substitute
- 5 medium chayote squash
- 1 ½ teaspoon cinnamon
- 1 tablespoon xanthan gum
- 1 tablespoon lemon juice
- ⅓ cup butter cut into small pieces
- ¼ teaspoon ginger
- ⅛ teaspoon nutmeg
- 2 teaspoons apple extract optional

Topping

- low carb sugar substitute
- 1 egg
- Instructions

Instructions

Crust

1. To make the crust dough, combine all of the ingredients.
2. Separate the dough into two balls.
3. Each crust ball should be rolled out into a pie crust.
4. In a 9-inch pie dish, place one of the crusts. Any cracks should be smoothed over.
5. Save the rest of the crust for the top of the pie.

Filling

1. Peel chayote and cut it into slices.
2. Boil the chayote slices until they are fork-tender. Drain. Return the pot to its original state.
3. Toss cooked chayote squash with cinnamon, ginger, nutmeg, sweetener, xanthan gum, lemon juice, and apple extract.
4. Fill prepared pie crust with chayote mixture. Using butter, dot the filling.

Topping

1. Cover the filling with the remaining pie crust.
2. Cut slits in the pie top and flute the edges of the pie crust together.
3. Brush the top crust with egg and, if desired, add more sweetener.
4. Preheat oven to 375°F and bake for thirty to thirty-five minutes.

KETO YELLOW SQUASH CAKE

Prep Time: 5 Minutes

Cook Time: 45 Minutes

Serves: 15

A delicious sugar-free dessert can be made with summer squash. This low-carb, gluten-free yellow squash cake is a custard-like cake with bits of squash.

Nutrition

Calories: 206 | Carbohydrates: 2.9g | Fiber: 1.1g | Fat: 20.3g

Protein: 3.8g | Sodium: 143mg

Ingredients

- 4 large eggs
- 13.5 ounces canned coconut cream coconut milk could also be used
- 2 cups yellow squash chopped and cooked
- 1 cup low carb sugar substitute or equivalent sweetener
- 2 teaspoons vanilla add more if needed
- ⅔ cup almond flour
- ¾ cup butter
- ¼ teaspoon salt
- whipped cream optional
- 1 tablespoon unflavored whey protein optional

Instructions

1. Peel, seed, and cut squash. To soften, cook for around twenty minutes in boiling water.
2. Stir the butter into the hot squash until it is completely melted.
3. In a large mixing bowl, combine the sweetener, vanilla, salt, almond flour, whey protein if using eggs, and coconut cream.
4. Fill a buttered 9" x 13" baking dish halfway with the mixture.
5. Bake for twenty-five minutes at 375 degrees Fahrenheit, or until golden brown and a toothpick inserted in the center comes out clean.
6. With whipped cream, it can be served slightly warm or cooled.

BUCHE DE NOEL – YULE LOG CAKE

Prep Time: 30 Minutes

Cook Time: 10 Minutes

Chill Time: 2 Hours

Serves: 16

A low-carb, gluten-free version of the Buche de Noel yule log cake. Holiday guests will never guess it's a sugar-free, low-carb dessert since it tastes so good.

Nutrition

Calories: 293 | Carbohydrates: 6g | Cholesterol: 140mg | Protein: 7g | Fat: 26g

Saturated Fat: 16g | | Fiber: 3g | Sugar: 4g | Sodium: 161mg

Ingredients

Cake

- 2 tablespoons dark cocoa powder
- 6 organic free-range eggs separated
- 1 tablespoon psyllium husk powder
- 3 organic free-range eggs whole ½ cup coconut flour 120 ml
- 2 teaspoons baking powder
- ⅔ cup Sukrin:1 160 ml
- ¼ cup heavy cream 60 ml

Filling

- ½ cup heavy cream 120 ml
- 1 packet caffeine-free instant coffee
- 8.8 oz tub mascarpone cheese 250 g
- ⅓ cup SukrinMelis 80 ml

Frosting

- 2 teaspoons orange peel from organic orange freshly grated
- 4 oz grass-fed butter 115 g, softened
- 8 oz full-fat cream cheese 230 g, softened
- 6 oz dark chocolate 170 g, at least 85% cocoa
- 3 drops orange essential oil
- ½ cup SukrinMelis 120 ml

Instructions

1. Preheat the oven to 375 degrees Fahrenheit
2. Using parchment paper, line a baking sheet or jelly roll pan.
3. In a small mixing bowl, combine the coconut flour, psyllium husk powder, cocoa powder, and baking powder. Make sure there are no lumps in the mixture. The mixture can alternatively be sifted.
4. The egg whites will be whisked until stiff peaks form. Set aside.
5. In a large mixing bowl, whisk together the egg yolks, whole eggs, cream, and Sukrin. Using an electric mixer, beat until smooth.
6. Mix in the coconut flour mixture until it is completely smooth.
7. Stir in the egg whites until they are completely smooth.

8. Spread the batter into a 1/2-inch thick rectangular-shaped rectangle on the baking sheet or jelly roll pan lined with parchment paper.
9. Bake for ten minutes, or until just done, in a preheated oven. If you overbake the cake, it will crack when you roll it.
10. Take the cake out of the oven. Place a wet tea towel on top of the cake and cover it with parchment paper.
11. Over the moist cloth, place another baking sheet. Invert the baking sheets, making sure they stay together as you do so.
12. Carefully peel away the parchment paper from the highest baking sheet. Replace the parchment paper on top of the cake gently. Cover the dish with a damp tea towel. Allow it to cool completely before using. Prepare the filling while the cake is cooling.
13. To make the filling, whisk together the heavy cream and the coffee granules. To get stiff peaks, whip the cream and coffee mixture together until stiff peaks form. Set aside.
14. In a medium mixing bowl, mix the mascarpone and SukrinMelis. Using an electric mixer, beat until frothy.
15. With a rubber spatula, carefully fold in the coffee-flavored whipped cream until smooth.
16. Evenly spread the filling on the cooled cake, without filling the edges, leaving 1/2 inch (1.2 cm) between them.
17. Using parchment paper, carefully roll the cake into a tight cylinder. Tightly wrap in a tea towel. Refrigerate for two hours before serving.
18. To make the icing, follow these steps: In a microwave oven or in a water bath, melt the chocolate. Mix in the orange peel and set aside to cool until the chocolate is lukewarm.
19. In a medium mixing bowl, combine the cream cheese, butter, orange essential oil, and SukrinMelis. Using an electric mixer, beat until the mixture is smooth and fluffy.
20. Pour in the melted chocolate mixture and stir until smooth with a rubber spatula.
21. Remove the parchment paper off the cake roll. Using the chocolate frosting, frost the cake. If the frosting is too stiff, heat it for a few seconds in the microwave.
22. After icing the cake, use a fork or a rubber spatula to make the surface look like bark. Cut the ends off and use them as projecting stumps on the cake roll. If desired, add additional decorations. Serve and keep the leftovers refrigerated. The next day's Low-Carb Buche de Noel is the greatest.

KETO JICAMA APPLE FILLING

Prep Time: 10 Minutes

Cook Time: 15 Minutes

Serves: 8

Many recipes use apple pie filling, which isn't low carb. Instead, a jicama apple filling, which is lower in Carbohydrates, can be used.

Nutrition

Calories: 129 | Carbohydrates: 6.1g | Cholesterol: 31mg | Fiber: 3.4g | Sugar: 1.2g

Protein: 0.6g | Fat: 11.6g | Saturated Fat: 7.3g

Ingredients

- ½ cup low carb sugar substitute
- 1 tablespoon cinnamon
- 4 cups jicama chopped
- 2 teaspoon apple extract
- 1 teaspoon vanilla extract
- ¼ teaspoon nutmeg
- ⅛ teaspoon cloves
- ½ cup butter

Instructions

1. In a pan, combine chopped jicama, butter, sugar, and spices.
2. Over medium heat, cook and stir until the jicama has softened.
3. Stir in the apple and vanilla extracts at the conclusion of the cooking process.
4. Warm the dish before serving.
5. Refrigerate for up to a week or freeze for up to six months.

STRAWBERRY ALMOND MILK CHIA PUDDING

Prep Time: 15 Minutes

Cook Time: 4 Hours

Serves: 4

This low-carb strawberry almond milk chia pudding is delicious. The fruity flavor is light and refreshing, and it's a great way to reap the chia seed advantages.

Nutrition

Calories: 111 | Carbohydrates: 3g | Cholesterol: 0mg | Protein: 4.4g | Fat: 1.8g

Fiber: 7.8g | Sugar: 2.3g | Saturated Fat: 0.7g

Ingredients

- 2 cups unsweetened almond milk
- 1 cup fresh or frozen strawberries chopped
- ⅛ teaspoon vanilla stevia drops
- ⅛ teaspoon monk fruit liquid extract
- 1 tablespoon lemon juice
- ⅓ cup chia seeds

Instructions

1. Stir chia seeds into almond milk in a medium mixing basin.
2. Combine the sweetener, lemon juice, and strawberries in a mixing bowl.
3. All of the ingredients should be thoroughly combined.
4. For the next fifteen minutes, stirring every five minutes.
5. Chill for at least four hours or overnight after dividing into serving plates.

CRANBERRY EGGPLANT BREAD PUDDING

Prep Time: 5 Minutes

Cook Time: 70 Minutes

Serves: 9

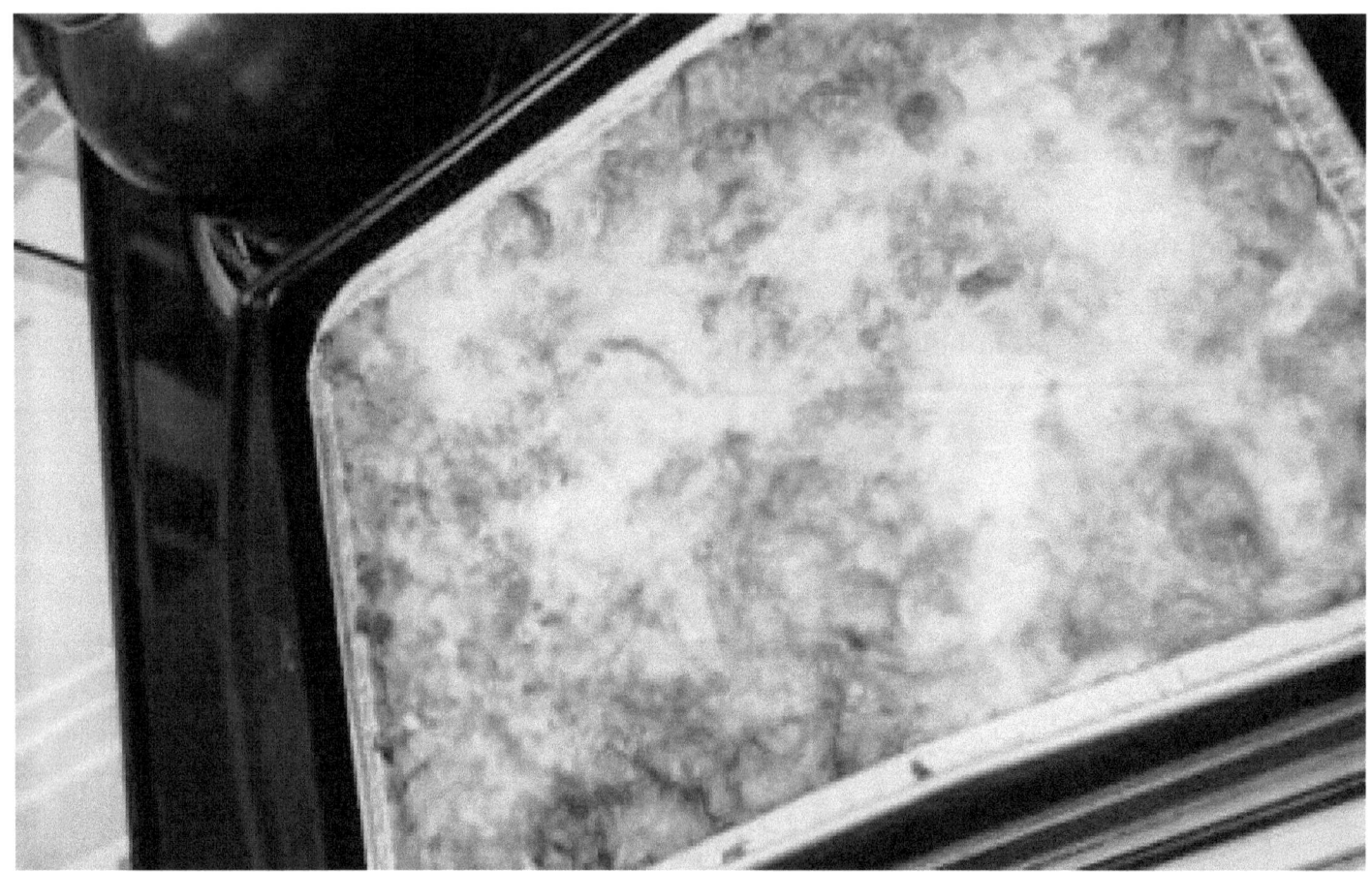

A delightful bread pudding with cranberries and eggplant. It doesn't contain any actual bread. Instead, eggplant is utilized, and you'd never guess it by the taste.

Nutrition

Calories: 221 | Carbohydrates: 6.5g | Cholesterol: 73mg | Fiber: 2.6g | Sugar: 3.7g

Protein: 4.5g | Fat: 21.1g | Saturated Fat: 17.5g

Ingredients

- 4 eggs
- 3 cups almond milk
- ¼ cup sugar-free dried cranberries
- 2 cups eggplant peeled and cubed
- 2 tablespoons butter melted
- 1 teaspoon vanilla extract
- ½ teaspoon cinnamon
- ½ cup Sukrin Gold
- pinch nutmeg
- pinch salt

Instructions

1. In an 8-inch or equivalent baking dish, arrange the eggplant slices.
2. Pour melted butter over the eggplant.
3. At 350°F, bake for fifteen minutes or until soft. Any excess liquid must be drained.
4. Combine the eggs, Sukrin Gold, vanilla, cinnamon, nutmeg, and salt in a medium mixing dish.
5. Blend in the almond milk until it is completely mixed.
6. Over the eggplant, pour the milk mixture.
7. Cranberries will be sprinkled on top and pressed into the liquid.
8. Preheat oven to 350°F and bake for forty-five to fifty-five minutes.
9. If preferred, top with whipped cream and serve warm or at room temperature. Refrigerate any leftover.

SIMPLE LOW CARB SUNDAE

Prep Time: 5 Minutes

Cook Time: 0 Minutes

Serves: 4

This low-carb sundae is a winner because of the delicious combination of chocolate, cream, raspberries, and coconut. After a meal, this dish is simple to prepare.

Nutrition

Calories: 457.9 | Total Carbohydrates: 8.6g | Carbohydrates: 5.2g | Sugar: 2.5g

Protein: 3.5g | Fat: 46.7g | Fiber: 3.4g | Sodium: 48.3mg

Ingredients

- 2 tablespoons granulated sweetener of choice or more, to your taste
- 500 ml (2 cups) double/heavy cream
- 1 tablespoon cocoa powder unsweetened
- coconut chips unsweetened
- 1 cup blackberries
- 1 cup raspberries

Instructions

1. Whip the cream and sweetener together until hard but not too firm, or the cream will separate.
2. Start by layering the whipped cream with the raspberries, blackberries, and shredded coconut in wine glasses or tumblers.
3. Continue to add layers that are pleasing to the eye. Set aside part of the whipped cream and mix in with chocolate powder.
4. More berries and chocolate whipped cream finish off the low-carb sundae.

www.ingramcontent.com/pod-product-compliance
Lightning Source LLC
Chambersburg PA
CBHW081417080526
44589CB00016B/2576